KEEPING THE RECORD
A Brief History of the Oxford Association of University Women, 1914-1994

KEEPING THE RECORD
A Brief History of the Oxford Association of University Women, 1914-1994

compiled and edited by
MABEL SAUNDERS

PUBLISHERS   **BOOKMARQUE**   TYPESETTERS

for

Oxford Association of Graduate Women
1994

Keeping the Record
Oxford Association of Graduate Women 1994

First published October 1994
© 1994 Oxford Association of Graduate Women

ISBN 1-870519-35-3

Illustrations: (1) courtesy of Mrs Thorn;
(2, 3 and 4) courtesy of Miss Vance;
(5 and 6) courtesy of Mrs Kirkwood;
(7 and 8) courtesy of Ian Rogers.

British Library Cataloguing in Publicationa Data

A Catalogue record for this book is available from the British Library.

Design & layout by Tom Colverson
Set in 11 on 13 pt Times
and printed on Bisley Antique Bookwove
Published by Bookmarque Publishing
Printed and bound by Antony Rowe Limited

*This book was produced as part of the
80th Birthday Celebration of the
Oxford Association of Graduate Women*

CONTENTS

xi

ILLUSTRATIONS

EDITORIAL

The years 1914-1994 have seen profound changes in the structure and functioning of society in this country. Among those changes that have had an incalculable effect on our lives, one of the greatest must be the recognition that women have brains and are capable of benefiting from higher education. This is true, not only of those who are academically gifted, but also of those who can be inspired by encouragement to raise their sights to greater aspirations.

When it was realized that the Oxford Association of University Women would be 80 years old this year we felt that this milestone should be marked. It was suggested that our members should contribute written accounts of their individual recollections of the era into a small book, and that this should be linked to a festive gathering in Oxford.

Our President, Mrs Nancy Trenaman, has been largely responsible for bringing this suggestion to fruition, by organizing the Seminar and lunch party at St Anne's College on October 1st 1994, and by undertaking the research that has produced the essay that deals with the early days of our Association.

The remaining contributions reflect individual responses to a free choice. Writers were asked to express their interest in any aspect of the period – changes in educational possibilities, widening employment opportunities, and looking outward to links with women overseas.

I am indebted to those members who have contributed their personal responses. The result could be likened to an Impressionist painting, where deft brush-strokes convey aspects of the age in which women were beginning to achieve their potential, particularly in education.

It is with great regret that I have to record the recent death

1

of Mabel Bennett, who contributed the 'Memory of Crosby Hall'. Her lively mind and perceptive comments will be much missed at our meetings.

My thanks are due to Miss Rachel Trickett, formerly Principal of St Hugh's College, Oxford, for allowing us to borrow the title of her talk 'Keeping the Record' for our book.

We are also grateful to the President of the British Federation of Women Graduates, Mrs Griselda Kenyon, for permitting us to use their shield and motto on the cover of our own publication. Finally, but by no means least, I wish to express my appreciation to Mr Tom Colverson, whose advice and practical help have been invaluable during the preparation of this book.

Mabel Saunders
Editor

KEEPING THE RECORD
A Brief History of
The Oxford Association of
University Women 1914-1994

At a preliminary meeting on 18th November 1913 the decision in principle was taken to establish an Oxford Association of University Women*. This was at the instigation of the British Federation (founded 1909) seeking to establish a network of local Associations across the country. The minutes of that meeting and of the first formal meeting in March 1914 convey the impression that the Oxford women considered that they had been a bit slow off the mark (though Oxford was the ninth Association to be founded).

At that time there were no selfgoverning women's colleges in Oxford. It was not until 1920 that women became members of the University and entitled to have the University's degrees formally conferred on them. But in the last quartile of the nineteenth century four Women's Halls had been established (Lady Margaret, Somerville, St Hugh's and St Hilda's) together with the Society of Oxford Home Students, subsequently St Anne's College. These provided residence for women students while the Association for the Education of Women in Oxford (AEW), founded in 1878, took care of their academic needs by appointing tutors, both male and female, to teach them. By 1913 there were many women so engaged: indeed, the preliminary meeting that year was convened by the Society of Oxford Women Tutors. So it is not surprising that the early members of the Association included many academic women and the wives of male dons who supported the AEW both financially and in spirit.

* Until 1992 the titles 'British Federation' and 'Oxford Association' ended with the words 'of University Women'. In May 1992 The Association substituted the words 'Graduate Women' and the Federation 'Women Graduates'. Since this short history covers a period of 80 years, for the sake of simplicity the original titles have been used throughout.

1914 was not, on the face of it, a propitious time to launch any new enterprise: less than five months after that first Annual General Meeting war was declared. However, both world wars had a profound, and on the whole, beneficent, effect on women's activities and prospects. Because they were needed to replace fighting men their efforts to achieve something like parity in pay and conditions, as well as taking on work hitherto reserved for men, received support which would probably not have been forthcoming in peacetime at that stage.

At a meeting of the Association in 1916, Miss Burrows (then Principal of St Hilda's Hall, and subsequently of the Society of Oxford Home Students) proposed a recommendation to the Federation to compile a Register of University Women to guide students about future employment. The Federation welcomed this: Miss Sargant (then President of the Federation) and Miss Burrows undertook the work in the early stages and paid its expenses. Although some women did find jobs through the Register – Miss B A Lees of Oxford who was appointed to a temporary lectureship in History at Manchester University was one – the scheme was costly in comparison with the results. In 1916 it was transferred to the Board of Trade but returned to the Federation in 1929, this time for administration by a secretary, the first paid employee of the Federation. The scheme was finally abandoned. Curiously enough, at the Association's AGM in 1918, Miss Pope and Miss Penrose – both of Somerville – expressed the view that the method so far adopted was mistaken: instead of questioning students about the kind of work they wanted, the aim should be to tell then what work was available. Miss Penrose suggested, as the mechanism, a system of Appointments Boards in each University. By the 1930s these were widely available, though this may be purely coincidental.

At the Association's AGM in May 1917 the question of

4

Compulsory Continuation Classes – a method of continuing education beyond the then school leaving age – was discussed, with Miss Annie Rogers, Secretary of the AEW's Committee in the lead. (Miss Rogers was a doughty fighter for women's education in Oxford. At the age of 17 she had sat the Oxford entrance examination, not open at that time to women. As she used only her initials and not her full name, it was supposed that she was a boy and two colleges offered her entrance awards, which they were obliged to revoke once her sex was identified.) None objected to the Continuation Classes as such, but Miss Rogers was concerned to ensure that if the scheme were adopted more women should be appointed to Local Education Authorities, that girls should be taught by women, that there should be a headmistress for the girls' education and that the headmaster should not have power to override her in disciplinary matters. A resolution on these lines was put to the Federation. In March 1918 a deputation (led by the Acting President of the Federation and including Miss Burrows (then President of the Association) waited on Mr Gilbert Murray of the Board of Education and came away with the impression that they had made headway. (Mr H A L Fisher, then President of the Board of Education, was thought to favour continuation classes as an alternative to raising the school leaving age.)

The General Meeting on 11 November 1918 (Armistice Day) naturally opened with expressions of deep relief at the ending of the war. Responding to an enquiry from the Federation about equal pay in industry and the professions, the Association expressed itself in favour of 'equal pay for work of equal value'.

Many questions were debated in the Federation and the Association during the war and the post-war period: women to be represented on bodies concerned with the teaching of Sciences; Solicitors (Qualification of Women) Bill; Burnham Scale; Criminal Law (Amendment) Bill; Summary Jurisdic-

5

tion (Married Persons) Bill; compensation for industrial injury – there were higher rates for men than women. Neither the Federation nor the Association was bashful in putting forward its views. For example in 1922 the Association instructed its Secretary to write to the Prime Minister protesting against the proposal to disband Metropolitan Police Women's Patrols. He turned her down but in the politest terms and, although the letter itself was typed, he signed it with his own hand 'Hugh Cecil' (The original is still in the Association's archives).

Generally speaking, the Federation's and the Association's views on the questions of the day seem to have coincided pretty well. But when in 1925 the Federation suggested that a list of women should be compiled as potential candidates for election to University seats in the House of Commons, Oxford demurred: better not to get into the business of Parliamentary elections. In 1918 the Leeds Association asked Oxford's opinion on the Federation's decision to raise the capitation fee without consulting the Associations. Oxford thought that the increase itself was justified but passed the following resolution:

> We are of the opinion that no important question should be settled either by the Executive or by a General Meeting of the Federation without sufficient allowance of time to the Local Associations for considering the matter.

One of the longest-running campaigns concerned the position of women Civil Servants. Many were recruited in the First World War but only at junior levels (though Miss Hilda Martindale, a former student at Bedford and Royal Holloway Colleges, London, became the first woman Inspector of Factories at about this time). Rank for rank their pay was lower than that of men. In 1917 on the suggestion of Miss Burrows, a woman Civil Servant was co-opted to the Executive Committee of the Federation because 'the position of woman

6

Civil Servants is at present engaging the attention of the Executive'. In 1919 the Federation sent a deputation (consisting of Miss Penrose, President, Mrs Smedley Maclean, Treasurer, Miss Burrows, member of the Executive) to the Committee for Recruitment to the Civil Service after the War. In reporting to the Association Miss Burrows commented 'In spite of some difficulty... in getting recognition of the particular points they wished to express, the general impression gleaned by the delegation was that the prospects of women in the Civil Service were improving'.

Progress was not conspicuously rapid. In 1926 women were for the first time allowed to take the examination for the Administrative Grade (First Division) of the Home Civil Service: two were successful on that occasion. Women were still paid at a lower rate than men and were required to resign on marriage. (One very distinguished woman Civil Servant of strong character got round the marriage bar by quite openly living with the man whom she married immediately after the abolition of the ban early in the Second World War). Permanent recruitment stopped in 1941 but many women joined the Service as temporaries and some of these sat the examination when permanent recruitment was resumed after the war. Women were not permitted to enter the Foreign or the Diplomatic Service until 1946. Equal pay was still in the future. It was not until 1955 that it was announced and introduced gradually (over a period of seven years, however). Still, it was a famous victory and the efforts of the Federation significantly contributed to the outcome.

Besides accelerating improved conditions for working women, the two World Wars made women more conscious of developments outside their own countries. Of course individual British women had travelled abroad before 1914, often as the wives of diplomats, less frequently on their own initiative. But after 1918 their journeys were increasingly in a representative capacity. In 1920 Dr Ivy Williams, Law Tutor at the Society of Oxford Home Students, was a delegate at the Hague Conference. In 1941 representatives of the Association at the BFUW's AGM heard an account by Professor Winifred Cullis of her wartime visits to America and the Far East commissioned by the Ministry of Information.

There must have been Belgian refugees in Oxford during the First World War but there is no reference to them in the Association's records. By the 1930s German (often Jewish) refugees were seeking asylum in Oxford: the University and the Colleges did their best to provide employment and accommodation. The Association appealed to its members to help refugees generally; and offers of accommodation, and in some cases domestic employment, were received during and after the war. The Association funded Miss Frieda Schreier, a refugee from Prague, for a degree course at the Society of Oxford Home Students 1939-42 and contributed to funds requested by the Federation to help refugees from Austria and Poland and especially for Polish women stranded in Siberia. After the war, when communications were restored, parcels of food and clothing were sent via the Federation to continental Europe. (During the war itself the generosity of the American, Canadian and South African Federations in sending similar parcels to Britain was greatly appreciated).

But the strongest, and longest-lasting, stimulus to international contacts was undoubtedly the emergence of the International Federation of University Women which was inaugurated in London by representatives of fourteen countries in 1920. The practice of meeting at regular intervals in a succession of countries has probably done more than anything else to increase our knowledge of other communities' problems and to establish personal friendships outside national boundaries.

It was apparently the custom at one time for delegates to IFUW meetings to take gifts to the hostess country. The minutes of the Association record that for the meeting at Helsinki in 1959 the Federation's Delegation bore with them some typical British prints, including one of Oxford.

* * *

The acquisition of Crosby Hall in 1926 followed hard upon the founding of IFUW (and both owed a great deal to Professor Caroline Spurgeon, President of the Federation, 1919-1924, and the first President of IFUW). Fund raising began in 1923. In 1955 the Association decided to 'name' a room in Crosby Hall in memory of Dame Emily Penrose (Principal of Bedford and Royal Holloway Colleges, London, respectively 1893-8 and 1898-1907, Principal of Somerville Hall and subsequently College, Oxford 1907-26, President of the Association 1914-16, President of the Federation 1919). The target, £1,000, was reached in 1964; subsequently further funds were gathered to furnish the room.

One hardy perennial subject for discussion in the Association has been money. The original subscription agreed in 1913 was set at two shillings and six pence (equivalent to 25 modern pence). Of this the sixpence was in effect an entrance fee, charged only in the first year of membership. The rest was divided equally between the Federation and the Association – one shilling each. There is no longer an entry fee and the annual subscription currently stands at £29, of which £28 goes to the Federation and £1 to the Association. Of course inflation is largely responsible for the huge increase overall. The proportions between capitation and the local share, however, have regularly led to discussion at the Association's AGM. Honorary Treasurers of other Associations may be comforted to know that successive Treasurers of the Oxford Association have frequently complained of late payments over the years.

In the earlier years there were often as many as four General Meetings a year of which the AGM was one. About once a year a general meeting was followed by a talk; for instance in 1924 Professor Spurgeon was urging young women to take an interest in finance and commerce – 'a side of public life which so far had hardly been touched by women'; in 1931 Miss Margery Fry (Principal of Somerville) spoke on penal reform; in 1938, Mrs Smedley Maclean spoke on the international aspects of the Federation's work. The Association was always glad to entertain visitors and involve them in any social activity which was taking place, from boating to buildings or gardens of interest, to theatre and music. Representatives of other Associations were invited to Oxford's annual dinner. A speciality which developed between the wars was conducted tours of Oxford Colleges, especially the grand and ancient, as well as the galleries and museums. Mrs Margaret Sainsbury (President of the Association 1976-9 and Vice-President of the Federation 1979-82) developed this form of entertainment to a fine art. Visitors from other Associations, the Federation's Executive Committee, Federations from overseas, individual students living at Crosby Hall, were all entertained in this way.

'I skip forty years', said the Baker, in tears. Not exactly; and no tears. Although clearly there must be diversity between the Associations, particularly on the social side, the fact is that the questions of the day which exercise the Federation also exercise the Associations and vice versa. According to the Oxford Association's minutes there were 28 Associations in 1944, but a great many more were added after that date. It follows that the closer one approaches the later years the greater the number of individuals across the country aware of the issues discussed. That is why this short history concentrates on the earlier periods.

Nancy Trenaman
President, OAGW

Grateful acknowledgement to Dr Marjorie Reeves, Honorary Fellow, St Anne's College, *An Informal History 1879-1979*, published 1979; and to Mrs Janet Howarth, Fellow and Tutor, St Hilda's College, for the chapter 'Women' in *The History of the University of Oxford*, Volume VIII, published 1994.

UNIVERSITY WOMEN IN UGANDA

It was not until my husband and I went to Uganda in 1966 that I had any connection with the Federation of University Women. When we lived in Bolton it was not practicable to join the nearest, the Manchester Association.

Having supported African schoolgirls for many years I thought a description of the African end of those awards might be interesting. Before our Zimbabwe students we had several Ugandans. I joined the Uganda Association partly because it provided a meeting-place for 'like minds' and also because its most significant activity was its link with the BFUW Scholarship Fund.

In Uganda everybody had to pay for their education. Even the youngest primary schoolchild was expected to take a few coppers each week. Then there was a hurdle to take before entering secondary school, and frequently those who qualified could not raise the necessary funds. Terrific efforts would be made for the first year's payment; relatives would be bombarded with requests for help, again frequently unavailing. This was, of course, (why 'of course'?) particularly the case in regard to girls, yet it was most desirable that educated men who could rise high to be lawyers or in the Civil Service, or as Head Teachers, should have wives who could fit into their new social status. But many bright girls had to miss a term or give up school entirely simply because there was no more money.

The BFUW scheme for helping schoolgirls was warmly supported by the Uganda Association, where there was a very mixed membership – British, Americans, Canadians, and of course a number of prominent Ugandans, both local and Asian.

The Scholarship that was set up was, I think, valuable, in

12

that it was designed not only to help the cleverest girls, but required them to be seriously interested in a career and of good character.

In the first place the Secretary wrote to the Heads of most of the Girls' Secondary Schools in the country, inviting them to put forward the names and report on up to three bright girls towards the end of their first year in the School. It would have been impossible to cope with the numbers if the girls had been involved at primary stage. These reports were then considered, and a short list chosen, by a sub-committee of UAUW. There had to be at least one Ugandan among the members of this sub-committee because it was felt that only their own people could possible appreciate the needs and pressures of the family.

The Warden of the Women's Hostel at Makerere University College gave hospitality to the candidates. Many had travelled by bus from remote schools, several hundred miles away, in order to reach Kampala.

The Committee had the School reports and the Headteacher's views, plus some knowledge of a girl's family. In the interview the candidate was encouraged to talk about herself and her family. Many of the parents were totally illiterate, so that school life represented a tremendous leap forward. Each girl was assessed on all this as well as on her academic standard and perceived potential. Many of them were well over normal first-year secondary school stage, possibly 14-15 years of age, having missed whole terms for financial and other reasons.

At the end of the day we tried to give some financial help to every girl who was called for interview. The girls were entitled to stay two or three nights at Makerere, according to their travelling times. One occasion was a salient example of how seriously the Ugandans themselves regarded the privilege of a scholarship. One girl decided to stay an extra night, without permission, in order to go into Kampala to

13

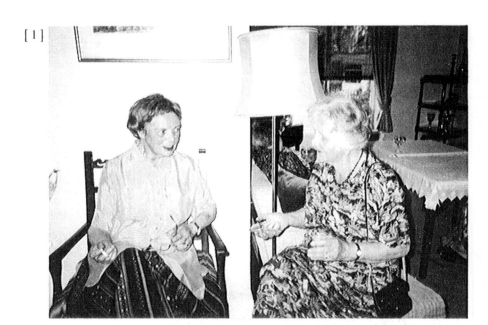

THE PRESIDENT'S PARTY 1994

(facing page, top)
Mrs Nancy Trenaman, President, (left) *talking to Mrs Margaret Poskitt.*

(facing page, bottom)
(left) *Dame Isabel Graham-Bryce reminiscing with Mrs Daisy Franklin.*

(right)
Miss Mabel Saunders.

(bottom)
(left) *Mrs Pamela Wilson with Dr Barbara Fisher.*

[3]

[4]

enjoy herself. When the Warden informed us of this I think the Europeans and Americans were disappointed, but would have treated the matter leniently. Not so the Ugandans, who said that a girl who behaved like that was not fit to have a scholarship.

Among other activities of the Association we held lunches rather as we do here, with a speaker. Numbers fluctuated – sometimes 10-15; at others 20 and above.

A number of the scholars eventually went on to University.

My first memory of the Oxford Association was a very warm letter from the Secretary, Doris Hackman, welcoming my 'transfer' and inviting me to join the Committee. I arrived for the monthly lunch in the English-Speaking Union building where I was immediately greeted by the President, Elizabeth Davis, who gave me a most warm welcome – a very auspicious start for me.

Margaret Poskitt

WIDENING EDUCATIONAL
OPPORTUNITIES FOR WOMEN

The Minutes of 1966 of the Oxford Association make reference to the fact that as soon as the scheme for assisting African pupils was announced the Association was eager to take part and began collecting money for it. It was, however, two years later, in 1968, before the first holder of the award was secured – AGNES NABUSA, a secondary school pupil in Uganda.

After three years, and the completion of her scholarship, Agnes was replaced in 1971 by another Ugandan, SARAH ZARAMBE, who was supported until 1974. By this time it was clear that the policy of the Ugandan government prevented us from supporting any further candidates there. In 1977 the Association sent the balance of the money to the Federation for the BFUW Africa Fund. In May 1980 the President of the Zimbabwe Association asked whether the Oxford Association could support candidates from that country. The first of these (from 1981) was BEAUTY MWAKO.

Nancy Trenaman

Phyllis Akred, who has been responsible for the smooth running of the scheme from the Oxford end, reports as follows:

In 1981, the Oxford Association sent a letter to Zimbabwe saying that we would like to help support a Zimbabwean schoolgirl. We were given the name of Beauty Mwako, a student at a Secondary School in Chepenga, whose father had been killed in the fighting. She was to take her 'O-Level' examinations in November 1982.

During that year Oxford sent parcels of books for the school library, and these were much appreciated by the Head-

17

Mrs Kirkwood delivers a calculator on behalf of OAGW to Beauty Mwako in Zimbabwe.

(below)
Beauty Mwako and her relatives in Zimbabwe.

[5]

[6]

master. Beauty passed her 'O-Level' exams well enough to proceed to take 'A-levels', but unfortunately her mother developed tuberculosis, and Beauty had to stay at home to look after the younger children whilst her mother was in hospital. She wrote to ask for summer dresses, which were sent from a number of members in various sizes, but we were assured that all of them were a good fit.

Eventually, instead of going to school and taking her 'A-Levels', Beauty became a student at the Belvedere Teachers' College in Harare. As her tuition fees were paid by the Government (to be repaid later) the Oxford Association offered to provide textbooks, of which there were very few in Zimbabwe – and those available were expensive. We were asked to provide a calculator and this Mrs Kirkwood kindly took to Beauty. A photograph shows Mrs Kirkwood and Beauty, the latter proudly holding aloft her computer.

Beauty, our first Zimbabwean bursary-holder, was an excellent correspondent. At first her English was rather halting, but it improved later, and was always genuine, unsophisticated and entertaining.

Beauty qualified as a teacher and continued to write to us until 1988, telling us of her husband and her daughter. Since then, we have helped MIMMY, TSHADIWA, EMILY and WENDY, but none for such a long time as Beauty.

We were delighted in March 1994 to receive a long letter from Tshadiwa, whom we helped in 1990, saying that she had finished her degree course in Pharmacy and was now taking a training year in a Government hospital. She intends to join the Zimbabwe Association of University Women, in order to help others in the way that she herself was assisted.

Phyllis Akred

*   *   *

19

Funds for the support of the Zimbabwean students come from several sources, one of which is the Annual 'Bring and Buy Sale' which has become a feature of the OAGW pre-Christmas Lunch. Sachets of pot-pourri made from each summer's flowers are sold on this occasion, and most of these are gathered and donated by Mrs Jane Hare, who has great sympathy with the cause of women's education in Africa.

It is pleasant to realize that fading roses from an English garden are bringing fresh hope to potential women students in Zimbabwe.

Editor

A MEMORY OF CROSBY HALL

I joined the BFUW in June 1930 after Schools while waiting for my viva, feeling that it would mark my graduate status and apparently certain that I should be successful. The Oxford Association of that day had sent round invitations to the women's colleges about the national and international federations and their activities and the facilities they offered. I was attracted and I joined.

After that I was kept in touch with but not near an active group, and as I was studying for the Lambeth Diploma as well as teaching full time I did nothing more about my membership than read anything I was sent. Then came the war, and after that I was asked to be Honorary Secretary for the Diploma, and this took all my spare time, as I was also resident warden of a students' hall of residence, as well as lecturing in Divinity.

One of my jobs as secretary was to organize the exam for the Diploma at the beginning of January each year, and I found out that Crosby Hall, which was much used by foreign students at that time, had rooms vacant, as many students were away over Christmas and the New Year. It was possible to book the library for the exam itself, to arrange for lunch for the candidates, and residence also it they wished it. Many did, as it saved them a cold and crowded journey each day.

Miss Buckmaster was Warden and she ran the hall as much on college lines as possible, with formal dinner in the medieval hall each evening. Food was still difficult in those years after the war, but the catering was good, considering the difficulties; I remember having yoghurt for the first time there. Cups of tea and coffee were provided for the candidates morning and afternoon. The arrangement worked to everyone's satisfaction. I used to attempt watercolours of the Embankment from the window of my room when I was not invigilating!

Then came another long interval when my contact with the Federation was slight. When I moved to Southampton I was transferred to a very active and welcoming association. They not only sent me notices of all their meetings, but a member would ring me up before each one to make sure that I intended to come. I found myself welcomed into a friendly and congenial set of women and soon became an active member, not only attending regularly but even taking office. I am still in touch with the friends I made then. When I came back to Oxford I found the same welcome and was able to enlarge my circle of friends. BFUW/BFGW stands for friendship for me.

F Mabel Bennett

OCTOBER 1934: SIXTY YEARS ON...

Mist from the river and sounding bells,
The curfew from Tom Tower
Is calling the scholars home,
The booms stern and compelling to unaccustomed ears.
But soon they will go unheeded, unremarked
By students with much else to see and hear.
A new life to be lived.

High up in the Clarendon Building
We read the Aeneid, Cicero and Tacitus
With Miss Lane-Poole: ebullient, strict, all-seeing.
'Straighten your academic caps', she said
Under Miss Hadow's mild and beneficent eye
We danced at the Randolph,
Joined the October Club, saw Hamlet at the OUDS,
And fell in love with Fortinbras.

Life for us was so good, friends so many,
Interests, night-long arguments sparkling with high hopes.
Essays were always in crisis, scrambled, half-done,
But the Radcliffe Camera was full of whispers
And joyful brief encounters.
There was no thought for the morrow, but all the same,
Feeling confident, poised, grown-up, we marched for peace.
World-wide the storm-clouds gathered. Friends left
To fight in Spain. While in Berlin the torches blazed
When they marched to the Horst Wessel,
But not for peace.

MISSION.   ERRATUM
To the jaunty, who wore them fashionably askew. "
Page 23, after Line 11, add

Magdalen Tower,
6am May Morning
1994.

(below)
Magdalen Cloisters,
May Morning 1994.

[7]

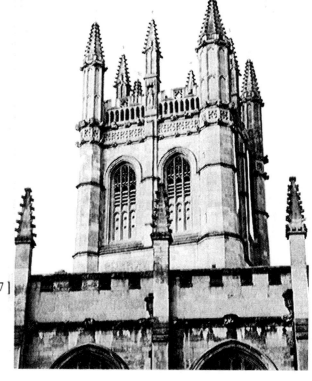

[8]

The world has grown old since then,
And memory blurs with age.
But nothing can rob the sound of the bells
From the mind or the heart. To this day
They echo a humble thanksgiving
For hectic, carefree, cloudless days
And starlit dancing nights.

Pam Wilson
March 1994

REMINISCENCES OF A GYMNASTIC HISTORIAN

In 1931 there were no County or State grants for anything other than strictly academic subjects. What I really wanted to do was to train as a PE teacher and to go either to Chelsea or to Dartford. My second choice – a very close second – was University.

In discussion with my headmistress I had asked what, as a PE Teacher, you did after 30? She gave her rare smile: 'You'd better ask Miss Pope.'

There being no money for PE, it was then a question of finding the means to go to University. My father had died when I was twelve and there were no widows' pensions in those days. Two possibilities lay ahead: a Kent major scholarship, depending on Higher Certificate results, and a place at the London Day Training College, now the Institute of Education. If you won your place there your fees were paid for three years at whichever college in London University offered you a place.

The whole thing hinged on a fairly lengthy interview with one of the staff. The Geography tutor – tall, thin, moustached and with a dry sense of humour – interviewed me. He was so like the treasured memories of my beloved father that I was instantly at home with him.

After much talk and sticking-on of little coloured circles to a large sheet of paper on his desk, the inevitable question:
'You say you read a lot – what have you enjoyed recently?' drove every title out of my head.
The Good Companions came to my rescue.
'Would you like to live in a caravan?
'I'm not sure. I think it might be difficult to keep clean and tidy.'
He smiled.

'I think you would manage' – and that ended the interview.

In those days the results of one's applications all came on the same day – February 1, if this was not a Sunday. Four long brown envelopes, and which one to open first? – the one I least wanted. It had no place for me. King's offered a place. So did London Day Training College, on condition that I pledged myself to teach for five years. All that remained was to gain the Higher School Certificate. Kent then gave me a grant and a loan, the loan repayment guaranteed by a farming uncle. That was no worry. I had worked out with my mother that I could manage on the grant.

Alas! for plans. The Wall Street crash of 1929, and the subsequent devaluation of the pound, led to the Geddes axe of 1931, and the halving of my grant, in the middle of my first year. I ended my four years with a £200 debt, and with too few jobs for too many teachers. Put on the Kent 'A' List of supply teachers, I was sent to a Girls' Central Scool in Bexley – Welling – where I had a testing five terms teaching mostly English and games.

Early in 1937 Queen Anne School, York, advertised for a junior historian able also to teach gym and games. I had taken a course in gymnastics in my fourth year, so I applied and was appointed. Later I realized that I was two for the price of one. The school had had an excellent report following a general inspection but a rider was added that both the History and PE departments were understaffed. Two for the price of one, and cheap at that! A year later, due for an increment of £12.00 per annum, I was informed by the York authority that as I had come to them from a Central School my increment would by £9.00.

Times have indeed changed. Cutting an increment by a quarter, regardless of qualifications, would result in a mighty protest now, if not a strike. No authority would attempt it. I took it on the chin, thankful to be employed.

Four years later and a new headmistress, an extra PE

teacher was appointed. I spent the next twenty-seven years teaching history and games, eventually as Senior History Mistress, with a succession of excellent juniors.

Contemplating early retirement in the mid-1960s and the wind of change in the educational world not being to my liking, a widower friend settled that for me. We married, and I came to Oxford. It took the Authority twenty years to determine the educational changes. Queen Anne Grammar School was to merge in 1985 with the local Secondary Modern School to become a school for 11-to-16-year-old girls.

At our final celebrations, (which I sub-titled 'Queen Anne going down with all flags flying'), a group from one of the most difficult forms I had taught invited me to join them at the tea-table. Just about the most awkward of them, as I remembered her, remarked:

'We weren't much of a hand at history were we, but what you taught us was good manners.'

On this happy note we drank, in tea, to Queen Anne.

* * *

As the Bard puts it:

> *There's a divinity that shapes our ends,*
> *Rough-hew them how we will.*

Daisy Franklin

A FELLOW-FEELING MAKES
ONE WOND'ROUS KIND...
David Garrick 1776

I cannot even remember when I joined the BFUW (in Huddersfield) – but it was soon after the end of the Second World War, probably in 1946. Certainly it was at the time when we had Utility Clothes and clothes coupons, and I was very impressed by a large parcel of clothes which came to us from one of the American Associations of University Women.

I think we shared them out according to fit, and I well remember trying on a summer coat which was a perfect fit and therefore became my property. I can see it now, a creamy-maize-coloured, full-length, edge-to-edge coat with a brown suede belt. It was in excellent condition and served me well for some years – in fact, I cannot remember being so attached to any garment before or since! I do not know which USA association it was, why they chose Huddersfield, or whether other associations sent to other towns.

This illustrates that University Women do not think only in high academic realms, but can also help one another in very practical ways.

Phyllis Akred

THE GODMOTHER SCHEME

The Godmother Scheme arose from the experience of Madame Hegg, Chairman of the IFUW Relief Committee. As she travelled in Europe visiting the Displaced Persons' camps she met women of various nationalities. Many of them were academic and professional women, now homeless and in distress, with no possessions and with no prospect of a return to a normal life, no profession and no hope.

Madame Hegg called on IFUW to make the utmost effort to help these women to return to life and hope. She set up the Scheme, sympathetically named, for the effort to be made was to take the form of a family relationship whereby IFUW would lavish on these outcasts the loving care of relatives. Homes had to be found, furniture provided and, over and above all these necessities, some form of income had to be found. Teaching, nursing and office work were suggested and training was given where necessary. Godmothers were encouraged to write frequently to their 'godchildren' and to provide little treats to break the monotony of the struggle. The call, as the prophet said, was: 'Awake! Take up your strength!'

The Oxford Association was quick to co-operate in raising funds and in contributing in practical ways. Recuperative holidays for their 'godchildren' were of great importance, and this was one of the beneficial activities that Oxford members provided. The help given by Oxford was invaluable and has meant a return to life for a number of women who were previously without hope.

Margaret Sainsbury

SECOND-CHANCE STUDENT

It will seem to have been a little late in the day – to start studying for a degree in the Humanities a year defore one's fiftieth birthday, but the Open University was created for late developers willing to apply themselves.

I had left a 'good' girls' school at the end of the 1939-45 War with a School Certificate after a year in the Sixth Form, but I wanted to busy myself and do something useful. During the next thirty years I trained and qualified as a nurse, married an RAF pilot, moved twenty-two times and brought up our three chldren. Studying along with them, I achieved two 'A-levels' as well as quite a lot of experience at home and abroad.

We settled for what promised to be a longish posting in a small Lincolnshire village of ninety souls, remote and seemingly tranquil. My elderly but lively-minded mother joined us there, but my children were at college or school, and more or less off my hands. There was a large, unkempt garden to tame. However, this was the time to apply myself to expanding my mind.

I enrolled with the Open University, and the first assignments of work reached me from the hands of the smiling postman. I had committed myself to the scholarly life – 'taking the plunge' was how I felt.

Open University degree courses involve 10-14 hours of study a week, which includes listening and viewing time. It had originally been named 'The University of the Air'. Qualifications to enrol were not demanded, and it really was intended to be open to all, but sadly it has become increasingly expensive since my days with it.

Each subject rating a credit is studied for thirty-two weeks, and six credits are required for a degree. Correspondence material is sent by post and further reading is suggested. One works at one's own pace. There are tests to tackle at home to help monitor progress, and written assignments, the results of which combine with a final examination. Personal tuition and counselling are given by part-time University and College teachers in each area.

I shared quite long drives to Nottingham or Lincoln with a couple of well-retired Service men. We travelled to our Seminars and Lectures and between-times met around my dining-room table for mutual support, encouraging one another and discussing our essays and assignments.

Then there were the Summer Schools. These last a week per credit, and during my study years I visited York, Cardiff and Kent Universities. It was both enjoyable and exciting to be given the experience of normal University life, if only briefly, and to share all those facilities. Most of all, getting together with others doing the same course was stimulating and rejuvenating.

As my courses were coming to an end my family faced another upheaval and moved to Oxfordshire. I did eventually get back to my books and became immersed in aspects of the English Civil War, so taking my last papers in the University of Oxford Examination Schools. How proud my long-departed father would have been could he have shared the news that I had earned my degree. He had hoped that I would achieve it in the conventional way, after my school-days.

My elderly fellow-students, Jim and Bill in Lincolnshire, told me of their success. It had been quite a long hard haul that changed my whole life.

June Thorn

THERE IS A TIDE...

When I left school in 1939 the storm-clouds were once again gathering over Europe. My headmaster, an Oxford man, who had taught me for School Certificate, had inspired in me a great love of English literature, but there were few opportunities for women to follow in his footsteps. Furthermore, war was imminent, and we must all pull our weight. Three weeks before the outbreak of war I started to train as a nurse. My dreams of reading English at Oxford were apparently to remain beyond the reach of any rational woman.

Twenty-five years later, having qualified as a nurse and as a midwife, I was the sister in charge of a busy surgical ward. The war with its attendant dramas was long over, and I had adjusted to living in a hospital world which was considered useful and left me little time to yearn for the impossible dream of an academic life.

Oddly enough, it was fatigue that seemed to work on my behalf. I had an afternoon off-duty, and spent two hours sleeping. I awoke, made a pot of tea, and turned on the radio. Someone should have sounded a trumpet! A woman who had just won a Mature State Scholarship was being interviewed. She was married with two children, and was going up to university with the full approval of her husband, who was prepared to look after the children to enable her to do this.

I was overwhelmed by this news and sought further information. It seemed that thirty Mature State Scholarships were offered annually by the Department of Education and Science. Successful candidates had to submit an extended essay, show proof of their ability to pursue the chosen course of study, and appear before a selection panel.

I did not hesitate for long. It would mean a tremendous change from the practical world of surgery back to the imaginative world of literature. Then, into my head came the remembered words from *Julius Caesar*:

There is a tide in the affairs of men,
Which, taken at the flood, leads on to fortune;
Omitted, all the voyage of their life
Is bound in shallows and in miseries...

After that there was no question of choice. I took the current when it served, was awarded a Mature State Scholarship, and came up to Oxford as one of the earliest post-war mature students, at the age of 45. A few years later, having completed a post-graduate Certificate in Education, I commenced work as a teacher of English in a large Comprehensive School. One of my responsibilities was coaching candidates for University Entrance.

Since then I have met several Mature Students and we have agreed that we valued very highly all the encouraging people who reached out to welcome us to Oxford. I remember particularly Dorothy Bednarowska, Kirstie Morrison, Elaine Griffiths, Patricia Ingham and the then Principal of St Anne's College, Nancy Trenaman.

The quality of their teaching, their concern and their forethought were kindly grappling-irons that bound us for ever to College in gratitude and affection. It is most fitting that the Year-Book of Senior Members of St Anne's should be entitled *The Ship*.

Mabel Saunders

OXFORD ASSOCIATION OF
GRADUATE WOMEN

Cover printed by Litho Impressions · Oxford